Generational Bondage:

Healing the Pain of the Past

Other Works by this Author

The following titles are available on Amazon, as well as Amazon Kindle.

The Family Set Free: A Journey of Deliverance and Healing

We are not wrestling against Flesh and Blood, but against powers and principalities. And this is true above all in our families. In this book or prayers, Fr. Joseph presents a twelve (12) day deliverance prayer model meant to help you and your family discover God's plan for your lives.

Seven Secrets of Failure: How Falling Down can Help you to Walk

This book is meant to help you overcome the temporary failures that come along the journey of life. The lessons contained here are necessary not just for some, but for all, especially for those caught in cycles of guilt and fear because of past mistakes. Ideal for parents, spouses, and especially for youth, its message is simple: where you end up has nothing to do with how much you fall down; it has everything to do with what you choose to do next.

Contents

Foreword

Fr. Cleophus Joseph has embarked upon the production of a selection of books aimed at helping individuals, families and communities deal with critical issues that affect people's lives today. The second of his works is a series of helpful material that would be useful in dealing with communication, stewardship, goal setting and prayer in the home. Following from this collection is a book on grief, where he outlines the importance of facing grief rather than denying it. These are meant to enhance and enrich family life and relationships.

I have no hesitation in granting an imprimatur to these works of Fr. Joseph, as he provides pastoral help and guidance for those who need it and seek it.

Robert Rivas O.P.

Archbishop of Castries, saint Lucia.

Introduction

What is baggage

Every person in every family carries baggage. On the physical level, when two persons decide to start a family, they leave the old home behind, but they carry clothes, utensils and furniture. This baggage can be positive: gifts given to the couple to start their new life. This baggage can also be negative; what they carry with them may be broken, or spoiled and sometimes, what they bring into the relationship can drive them apart. Imagine a family that is constantly fighting over the old sofa that the woman has placed in the living room. It may have sentimental value for her, but for whatever reason, it is a source of conflict in her new home. On the psychological level, emotional baggage is the same way. When we leave home, we take with us values and ways of interpreting the world; these values may have served us in our old home, but that does not mean that they belong in our new environment.

Baggage really is a neutral reality; there can be good baggage- that is the good and healthy notions that I learned, as well as unhealthy baggage: the negative, destructive values that I learned. In this book however, I will use the term to denote the negative. Negative Baggage is just another way of saying, "Generational Bondage" or "Generational Curse".

How this book came about

I have a naturally curious mind (maybe too curious sometimes). When I see something, I always want to know why it happens. Growing up, part of my interest was trying to understand why people do the things that they do. Especially, I was curious as to why someone who seemed to have everything going for him or her, would keep repeating the same mistakes. And it became even more interesting when I would often learn about that person's family history; then I would see the pattern being repeated over generations.

I resisted the idea of behaviours, illnesses and life circumstances being the result of God paying the parents in the children; after all, the bible clearly teaches against generational curses in terms of God punishing people for the sins of their ancestors (Ezekiel 18:2-20). But I do believe that our ancestors actions will have consequences on how we live today, materially, emotionally, in terms of our family reputation, and spiritually. But how, and why did people not simply break the pattern?

I looked at many theories. Among them were concepts of learned behaviour, parent wounds, psychological projection, demonic attachment and even genetics. Now, do not be confused; I am by no means an expert in any of these topics; I simply read much of the material about their effect on behaviour, much of which I could not understand.

I then became acquainted with the work of the Catholic Warrior,[1] Healing the Family Tree[2] and the Healing of

[1] Robert Abel. The Catholic Warrior. Valentine Media. https://www.catholicwarriors.com/index.htm. 2016. Web.
[2] Kenneth McAll. Healing the Family Tree. SPCK Publishing. 2013.

Families.[3] Bringing all this work together, I am more convinced that generational baggage is not simply a psychological and emotional issue, nor is it simply a spiritual issue, but that it involves healing in all these areas. The aim is to help the one doing the exercises to take full responsibility for his or her life and then to begin to live the fullness of life that God desires.

How to use this book

<u>One chapter at a time</u>

Firstly, like the other books that I have written, this is not simply for reading. The intention is that the persons take time to do each chapter. I recommend setting a weekend aside and going through a chapter with its exercises. This would make an interesting healing weekend retreat or seminar.

Kindle Edition.
[3] Fr. Yozefu SSemakula. <u>The Healing of Families</u>.
healingoffamilies.com. 2012.

Another way one can do it is to set aside six evening in a week, and coming together in a small group to do one chapter every evening.

Again, a group can set aside one particular day of the week, such as a Wednesday evening, and meet for six weeks to finish the material. The important this is to have a plan for doing the exercises that is convenient.

Do not do this alone

Now, there is nothing that says that you cannot do this project on your own (except the heading of this particular section). It is possible that you are very motivated and driven and that you can actually hold yourself to the standards that you want to change. So, it is not a sin if you do this alone (or at least not a serious sin).

I however, recommend that you do this with a group of persons -either friends, family, church members- who are interested in becoming better. In this way, you can be accountable to each other.

If you are doing this exercise with your family, I recommend that you write down the answers with yourself first, and then share with the rest of your family afterwards, chapter by chapter. Do not try to do more than one chapter at a time.

Doing this as a group seminar/retreat

If you are doing this workshop as a seminar with other families, then I suggest that you divide for this section into two groups: all men together and all women together. Appoint a group leader who will control the pace of the session as well as explain the questions if there is any difficulty in understanding. After finishing the exercise, have the group discuss the answers. Ensure that everyone gets a chance to speak.

I recommend the separation of sexes for the seminar for a reason: if there are persons who have been married for more than four years, they may not be communicating as well as they should. By journeying with the same gender, it is more likely that you will be able to share openly.

I do not necessarily recommend this section for children below age fourteen. I have never done such a session with persons below this age, so I am not sure how it would work at this time.

Things that you will need to consider

Writing material

You should provide, or ask the participants to bring along paper or a notebook, as well as pens or pencils for writing. You should also provide envelopes.

Altar area

For the fourth session, there should be a special altar, which could just be a small table covered in white tablecloth with two candles on it. You may also provide candles for all the participants, pr ask them to bring one along.

Counsellors and pastors

If you are working with a group, it may be wise to have counsellors available as some of the memories uncovered could be quite painful.

You may also invite a pastor or priest to journey with the group. On the final day, I recommend that the married couples renew their marriage commitment. If this book become part of a regular programme for families, that means that couples will be renewing the covenant to each other several times every year.

Who to invite to do this encounter

When setting up a group, one can invite all these persons to be part of the same session; just realise that they have different needs and the way in which the final sessions end will have to be worked accordingly.

Marries couples, especially newly married

The series is designed especially to help married couples and their families. Therefore, ensure that couples are invited.

Many young couples complain that the church does not create many opportunities for information and formation available to them. Persons desiring to do this as a seminar can contact the recently married couples in the parish or area and invite them to be part of it.

Engaged couples

This could be a wonderful resource for engaged couples, who are on the way to being married. They will get an opportunity to know themselves and their future spouses better.

Divorced and separated persons

It could be a great resource for divorced and separated persons. It could help move them to a place of deeper healing and self-discovery.

Couples that you wish to talk about marriage to

If there are couples who have been together for a very long time, are not yet married, but are not averse to the idea of getting married, they can be invited to do this programme as part of their formation. Persons often delay making a long term commitment out of fear; if they know that both they and their partner are committed to a process of emotional growth and spiritual, it may make the difference for them.

Persons discerning a vocation

Even if a man or woman is not looking to get married, but may be thinking about consecrating himself or herself to God in the single state, this would be a great resource. The more he or she discovers and loves self, the greater the gift of self he or she can be offer to the faith community.

Single persons looking to grow personally

One can also invite persons who may not be looking into any particular vocation, but who simply want to grow more, spiritually and emotionally, and who wish to attain deeper levels of personal healing.

Chapter 1:

The Image of a Healthy Family

He who finds a good wife finds happiness, a precious treasure granted by the Lord (Proverbs 18:22).

Christian Marriage: The Instrument of Bringing out the Best Version of Myself

How would you define family? There may be some funny cartoon out there that would say it is a prison or an asylum. That is the way we often see marriage defined on media; it s romantic at the beginning but it turns sour as time goes on. Watching people make fun of family may be funny on the big screen, but in real life, it is dangerous and painful. So how would you define family? Because what you think about family will control how you live it. If your definition is sound, your family will probably be a place of love; if your definition is harsh, then your family will probably be a lonely and painful reality. Especially if you are a parent or spouse, your family will be whatever you think it is.

So what does a healthy family look like? I believe that there are three dimensions to the answer of this question. Firstly, I like the way Matthew Kelly defines the Catholic worldview: it is about helping people become the best version of themselves that is possible.[4] It means that I will be the best man, or the best woman that I can be for you, and I will love you into being the best that you can be. If I want to have a good and healthy family, it cannot be about me; there is no room for selfishness or lone rangers in family.

Marriage and family is meant to make you a better version of yourself. That does not mean that just because you are married, that you will become a better person; it is not automatic. In my relationship, I can choose to learn

---

[4]Matthew Kelly. *The Four Signs of A Dynamic Catholic: How Engaging 1% of Catholics Could Change the World.* Beacon Publishing. 2013. Kindle Edition.

patience and gentleness to the faults of my partner; I learn unconditional love by being present to my children, even when they are behaving badly. You see, it is easy to overlook the offenses of a stranger; overlooking such offenses does not make me a patient person. It is when I can be gentle with those in my home that I have truly become patient. I honestly believe that family is God's greatest gift to us to teach us how to be saints; how sad we do not appreciate this gift.

The definition of a good husband or wife has little to do with how handsome or pretty he or she is. It is about whether I am being the best man or woman I can be in order to show you, my spouse that I love and appreciate you. The litmus test for your contribution to your family is, by the way you are acting right now, is it easier for the other persons in your family to be happy, healthy, intelligent and loving? And if the answer is "No," then something is wrong with your contribution to your family.

Now, this is a lot easier when couples have just met and

fallen in love. Falling in love puts you on an emotional high and you treat your partner with respect, love, admiration and gentleness. Few people are monsters in the courting stage of their relationship. You could spend hours on the phone talking, sometimes about nothing in particular. Every cent you had would be spent on flowers or chocolates to show how much you care. You maybe even went down on your knees, not only literally with the engagement ring, but figuratively, to show your admiration for the other person. So what happened? Are you and your spouse still close, and if not, where did the love go?

And again, if you have children, when your first child was born, you probably went crazy every time the child cried, and would run to make sure that everything was okay. You went out of your way to show your new angel to all your friends and family. You were so proud of your child's first words and you would listen intently to every syllable of "Mama" and "Dada". Do you still make time to listen to your child today? And if not, what happened?

Sometimes in relationships, **one person** changes dramatically and the whole relationship goes into chaos. This is especially true of relationships where there is physical and emotional abuse. Most times however, I have found that all members of the family simply draw apart. There are small things we all can do that we simply take for granted. Looking at another family from the outside, we would probably say, "You should not do that," or "Stop shouting at your spouse and insulting him or her," or "Stop treating your children as if they are not good enough," or "Stop being disrespectful to your parents." But we often cannot see ourselves doing these things.

If someone asks why my family is falling apart, I will blame my father, or my mother, my spouse or my children. I may even blame others outside the family: it is my boss' fault, or it is my best friend's fault. The truth is, it is all of is in the relationship; it is our fault. And if I am not doing the best that I can, if I am not doing what I am supposed to do, it is my fault.

So, do you show love and respect for your spouse? If not, whose fault is that? Do you make time for your children? If not, whose fault is that? When was the last time you did something to show your family members that they were important to you? And whose fault is that? When was the last time I apologised when I was wrong, or I forgave someone from my heart who apologised? And whose fault is that? If I am not doing my best, as a father or mother, husband or wife, brother or sister, then it is my fault; I am responsible.

Marriage is a Sacrament

The traditional way of speaking about Catholic Marriage is that it is a Sacrament. A sacrament is many things: it is an outward sign of grace working within us; my own personal definition is that it is a spiritual union between God and God's people. In every sacrament, God unites with us and does something to lead us to deeper holiness. So, in every Catholic marriage, we ask God to provide grace for our lives, the grace to live a life of unity together before God; the grace to find happiness with each other; the grace to raise children in love.

Because it is a Sacrament, it is also a covenant. It is a covenant between two people before God and it is the greatest symbol of God's love for His people. Because of this Jesus says that once it is done properly, it becomes unbreakable (Matthew 19:3-9). That is the reason why God hates divorce (Malachi 2:16).

The sacramental view of marriage is that man and woman are like Christ and His Church. Wives are called to be submissive to their husbands as the Church is to Christ. In our culture, this often seems to be degrading to women; but that is because, people often miss the next part. Husbands should love their wives as Christ loves His Church, laying down His life for her. I am sure that more women would be more than happy to be submissive to their husbands if they were convinced that their husband would lay down his life (and may by occasionally, his television remote and bottle of beer) for her, but that is just an aside. So, if a gunman walks into your house and is about to open fire, because you are the husband, you so love your wife the way Christ loves His Church, you will give your life for her and your family. And if you laughed at the idea, then you missed the part of marriage being a sacrament; sacraments require sacrifice. And of course, the idea of sacrifice also covers the other members of the family. How will you know that you can lay down your life for your family? Simple; if you can sacrifice your time, your energy, your affection, your pride, every day, then if the moment ever came, you would be able to sacrifice your life.

As a sacrament, marriage is founded on love, because God is love (1 John 4:8). Love is not easy; it is sacrifice. St. Paul gives us a lovely hymn to what love is: Love is **always** patient and kind; it is not jealous or vain; love is not rude or self-centred; it is not quick tempered, but is ready to forgive. Love is not happy with pain or wrong but delights in truth. Love never fails (1 Corinthians 13:4-8). Do you really love? Does your spouse or children know that they are loved? Because, even if you were the best speaker or singer in the world, if you speak without love, you are only a drum making noise. And if you had a thousand degrees in all subjects known to man (and occasionally woman); the most intelligent person alive, yet without love, you are nothing. And if you gave your spouse a new SUV for her birthday every year, and gave the in-laws a new flat screen television and gave the children a holiday around the world, you have given nothing (cf. 1 Corinthians 13:1-3). People know when your gifts are without love; they feel the emptiness in your giving. Who cares what you give? If you cannot give love, you can keep your gifts because in the end, they will not be appreciated. The only gift you can give that will truly matter is your heart.

Reflection Exercise

1. How would you describe marriage and family? And what is your family like?

2. What would you like marriage and family to be like?

3. Describe the way I treated my partner when we were courting? How did I show him or her that I cared?

4. How long have we been together?

5. How am I treating my spouse now? Have I become a better mate or am I becoming worse?

6. If my family members were to be honest about the way I treat them, would I be proud of what they would have to say about me? How does my family compare with Paul exhortation in Colossians 3:18-21?

7. How do I sacrifice myself for my family?

8. What ways do I show love?

9. What one thing can I do to become a better husband/wife/parent/brother/sister/child?

Chapter 2:

What Baggage?

The Lord is a faithful God who keeps covenant to the thousand generation of those who love Him and keep His commandments (Deuteronomy 5:9).

At some point in time, you either consciously or unconsciously decided on particular images of yourself. These ideas and concepts literally control your behaviour: **your actions in any area of life, relationships, conflict, work, and all the different facets of life, will almost always be consistent with your image of yourself in that area.** Many of our concepts about relationships are carried over from the relationships of our parents and other significant relationships when we were growing up.

For better or worse, the first place where a boy learns to be a man is by watching how the important men and women in his life, most often father and mother, deal with the issues of adulthood, such as respect, love, authority, fidelity, responsibility and emotional openness; and of course, the same is true for a girl. We will look at this again, but briefly, a boy sees the way his father treats his mother and his first unconscious thought is, "That is the way a man treats a woman." And he sees the way his mother treats his father and he will say, probably unconsciously, "So that is how I should expect a woman to treat a man."

What type of person are you? If you are a spouse, what type of husband or wife are you? If you are a parent, what type of father or mother are you? The things you struggle with, and we all struggle with some things, why did you learn to do those things?

Now, you are probably wondering why I said, "why" you learned the things you struggle with instead of where you learned them from. The reason is, sometimes, you may not carry the same dysfunction as your parents and grandparents; but unless you learned to break the cycle, you are definitely carrying the consequences. For example, my father was an alcoholic; I may never drink a single day in my life, but because I was dealing with a lot of embarrassment, I may have a volatile temper. Or my parents may have argued a lot and I am extremely timid, but I stammer. You may look at me and say that I broke the cycle, but all I am doing is manifesting the issue in a different way.

What might I be Carrying

Sometimes, the sins and bondage of our ancestors still affects us today. We find ourselves repeating their mistakes or carrying similar health issues and habits. Generational bondage simply means that there is an unlearned lesson passing down from generation to generation. Unlearned lessons come in many forms: for example, my grandfather four generations down was an alcoholic and adulterer. Because children learn what they see, his children look at his life and they decide what value to attribute to it. They can either learn the lesson from the pain they experienced and move on and heal, or they can get stuck in the cycle of repeating his mistakes.

Bondage or sin can be passed on by **modelling:** we repeat what we see our ancestors do. It is almost as if we decide, consciously or unconsciously, that we will be like our parents: that we will do the things we saw them do and act the way we saw them act. We do to our children what they did to their children, for better or worse, and we treat our spouses the way they treated each other, for better or worse. Or, we marry someone who will treat us the way an abusive parent treated the other. The interesting thing about this is that sometimes, we can absolutely hate our parents and the things they did to the family, yet we still seem to get stuck in this cycle. Some people whom I counsel, when they begin to tell me what they struggle with, I often ask them if they had a parent who struggled with the same issue, and almost always, the answer is yes.

There is a particular manifestation that I find intriguing: we can find ourselves doing what our ancestors did, even if we never knew them or saw them doing it. I saw this happen in children who had been adopted; even when they did not know their parents and family of origin, the adopting family could see that their actions were very much like that of their families. I have no idea how this unconscious transmission works, but I do know that generational bondage simply means that somehow, we are chained to our ancestors pain cycles.

Bondage or sin can also be passed on as a **consequence:** in this case, the things our ancestors did have caused cycles of pain in our lives. One of the easiest examples that I witness daily is a cycle of poverty. An ancestor who either does not know how to manage finance may pass on his or her debts to descendents. If these do not learn the lessons of proper financing, they in turn live in poverty and pass on the debt to their children. Now, we should make the point that not all this baggage is intentional; sometimes, someone may have planned well, but illness or a disaster occurred that completely erased the security they built. They will still pass this on as baggage to their descendents. Hopefully though, they will also give the values and standards to overcome it.

Where does the baggage come from

Some patterns can be seen for generations. I think of the example of Alice: she has a teenage daughter that she worries is starting to experiment with sex and no matter what her mother says, she is convinced that she is in love. I notice that Alice is a young mother, so I ask a few questions. It turns out, her mother had her while she was in her early teenage years; her boyfriend at the time refused to accept responsibility and left the young mother to fend for herself. Alice's mother did not know how to take care of her, so she sent her to live with her grandmother. Grandmother, who herself had her first child before she was married, and who had eight (8) children with different fathers, was not too materially well off. She was strict with Alice, trying to shield her from friends and relationships. But Alice was a bit of a rebel, probably because she felt angry at being abandoned by her own mother.

Alice had her daughter when she was fifteen (15). Alice's daughter is now seventeen and she is facing a family pattern that goes back at least three generations. Now, the daughter's life is not determined; she can recognize that she is very close to taking up this baggage and decide that she will not end up in a similar situation. And that is perhaps the saddest fact about baggage: that although it can destroy our lives, as well as the lives of our children and grandchildren, at any point in time, someone can always choose to break the pattern; it is sad because in many cases, the pattern continues.

Some patterns are picked up from the experiences of those around us. We see the actions of neighbours, television personalities and the culture around us. Depending on whether we respect the persons involved or not, we can then decide whether what they do is something we ourselves should be doing. Do you know the number of things we do, that we have no reason for doing except, "This is what my mother did," or "This is how my father did it." Or sometimes, in reverse, "I saw my neighbour doing this and I do not like my neighbour, so I will not do it." If you were to honestly look at some things, such as, off the top of your head, what are the things that scare you? If I ask you why they scare you, what would your answer be. I used to be afraid of rats because my mother was afraid of rats. I have yet to have a single negative experience being attacked by a rat, but even a dead rat could terrify me. Until I began to ask the question, "Why do I really feel this way?" I had no logical answer to that question; I have since learned to not be so afraid (just a little bit).

Another funny example from my life: when I was about five years old, my cousin, who was only one year older and whom I loved and respected, told me that I should not eat fish head as this could make me stupid. Children seem to know lots of things by simple intuition, right? I doubt that my six year old cousin ever did an experiment on the effect of fish head-eating and stupidity. In fact, I am not even sure that my cousin does not eat fish head; I was told that this may have been a ploy to keep all the fish head for herself. But I do know that from this time to now, almost thirty years, I have never eaten fish head; I still cannot bring myself to eat it today. That is a silly learned lesson, a bit of my baggage. It is basically harmless, and I do not really want to taste fish head as it may taste bad, right.

And here is another truth that baggage does: when we recognise that the original reason why we do something is faulty, we may find different reasons to keep holding on to the pattern. So, even if I see many other (and I believe but I cannot prove) rather intelligent people enjoying a good fish head stew, I probably will not like it because it tastes bad; and besides, the bones may get stuck in my throat (that's my reason and I am sticking to it). If however I was starving and the only thing to eat was fish head, then I would probably let go of it. In other words, we normally keep our baggage until we are forced to let go.

Do You Know What You Are Carrying

Baggage can be dangerous; because we often do not even realize that we are carrying it, it can control our lives today. Imagine, you may be oppressed by the pains, sins and failures of a thousand generations past. And because we cannot see it and it controls our lives, we often pass it on. Imagine that you will pass on to your children all the garbage and pain from a thousand past generations that have been destroying your life today.

But you do not have to carry baggage anymore; you can decide to break the cycle. And your children do not have to be slaves of the past anymore; you can teach them to be free. If you are to be successful in a relationship, you need to know what you're bringing to the relationship. Until you speak something out, you may never know that it's there.

We learned many different ways of behaving and thinking from our parents, from what they told us and especially from the way they acted. So if a parent is a compulsive gambler, then we may develop the habit of gambling ourselves. If we don't, then if we do not recognise it in ourselves, we can work with a compulsive gambler or marry a compulsive gambler. But one way or another, unless we deal with the brokenness we inherit, we will carry our parents unlearned lessons until we have understood and integrated the lesson ourselves.[5]

Now, remember, baggage can also be positive. We may have seen our parents being hard-working and generous, perhaps even to a fault. Take time to acknowledge the good. Otherwise, you may find yourself doing it without knowing why, and if anyone ever questions it, because you do not have a valid reason, you may give up something that is good. Remember, it will not always be easy to do what is right, but you need to do good because

---

[5]Jarema, Fr. William. Clergy Pastoral Institute. Archdiocesan Clergy Retreat. Cardinal Kelvin Felix Archdiocesan Pastoral Centre. September 2012. Talk.

it expresses the type of person you want to become. So be thankful for the good that you received.

Reflection Exercises I

1. Who would you consider are the three most important persons that you look up to (this can include parents, neighbours, celebrities, historical figures, etc.)?
    a. What have type of person were they? What did you learn from them?
2. If you were the one living their lives, what would you do differently?
3. If they were present with you today, what would you not want them to see you do? What things would you be proud to let them see you doing?

Exercise II: Acknowledging the Good

1. In your opinion, what are the most important things that make for a healthy relationship (ways of thinking and ways of acting)? Write down as

many as you can think of; try to get at least ten (10).

e.g. love _____   sex _____

_____   _____

_____   _____

_____   _____

_____   _____

_____   _____

2. In each of the above cases, discuss the following:

    a. Why do you think that this is important?

    b. Who taught you this value?

3. Were your parents together? If yes, then discuss the following:

    a. Were they married?

    b. Was the relationship happy or were they miserable together?

4. Write down a few things that they did (ways of thinking and ways of acting) that helped their

relationship, or some of the good memories you have of your family.

e.g. Parents went to church together..., mother cooked a good meal on weekends..., etc

_____

_____

_____

_____

_____

_____

5. Write down the positive things that you should do like your parents in your relationship

_____

_____

_____

6. Other people, such as neighbours, friends, or even television personalities, have left us examples by their own lives. What positive experiences or

affirming life lessons did I learn from persons other than my parents?

_____

_____

_____

_____

7. What are the positive things that your parents, or other significant adults in your life, did that you find yourself or your spouse now doing in your relationship?

_____

_____

_____

The truth is, if you are married, or to be married, then much of your sense of self worth is attached to how you contribute to the happiness of your family, especially your spouse. No normal man, just married for a year or two, wants to tell his friends how unhappy his wife and children are; as marriage lasts for a while longer, then that becomes a habit, but in the early years, you feel a great sense of importance in being able to say that your family is happy. If you know that good that your parents did, the positive things they passed on to you, then you have a pattern of behaviour that you can follow. The good memories that you have are ways in which your parents taught you to be a good man or woman. Ideally, your father or mother taught you, through these patterns, how to develop a positive self-esteem.

If it is hard to remember any positives, it probably means that there are many painful memories and that you need to forgive father or mother. No matter how bad anyone is, there is always something good in them. But the longer we are exposed to pain and abuse, after some time, it becomes easier to see only the bad. I do not know what you had to go through, but I do know that if you want to be healed, you need to have the courage to see both good and bad. If it is really painful to even attempt to see the good in a parent, then I suggest that you do The **Forgiveness Ritual** *at the end of* **Appendix I**, *and* *then come back to this exercise, but do not run away from the pain. The pain only grows when we ignore it; no matter how bad it is now, it will get worse if you do not face it.*

When the exercise is complete, everyone in the group can join hands and pray the prayer of thanksgiving together.

Prayer of Thanksgiving for Gifts Received

Lord, I thank you for the gift of my family. I thank you because from my family, many of Your gifts flowed to me. I thank You for these gifts and I ask that I may carry them forward in my new relationships. Lord, may I be the type of husband/wife that will encourage and lift my spouse. May I be the type of father/mother that my children need me to be. May I aspire to be the kind of man/woman that would make Your proud to call Yourself my Father. Amen.

Chapter 3:

Dealing with Negative Bondage

Lord, on account of our sins, and the sins of our ancestors, we have become a reproach... but O Lord, hear and pardon, for the sake of Your own name

(Daniel 9:16, 19).

What bondage may look like

Sometimes, I see baggage in the form of sins; I call these unlearned soul lessons. These can include adultery, stealing, lying, and others. So, you may know someone whose father or mother is known to have stolen. The child also develops into a thief. The parents did not say, "Come son, or daughter, let me teach you how to grow up to be a thief." The child simply learned the lesson because the parent never renounced it. Sometimes, baggage may come in the form of negative habits; I call these unlearned heart lessons. These could include smoking, alcoholism, drug use and spousal and child abuse. And sometimes, baggage may take the form of illnesses, unlearned body lessons. Some of these diseases are genetic, in which case, the person has to learn to manage themselves well in order not to contract it. But some of these diseases are lifestyle choices, which means that the person could easily have not gotten sick if he or she would change the way of life.

Sometimes we repeat the mistakes of the past because we think that it was okay to make them. We may know that it is wrong, but we justify ourselves; "My father used to do this so it is okay." Well, if you know that it was wrong when your father did it, then it is most probably wrong when you do it. And sometimes, we repeat the mistakes of the past because we pretend that we are better than our ancestors and therefore cannot fall in the areas where they were weak. For example, a man with an unfaithful father may decide that she is stronger than his father. So he is in a committed relationship, but he does a little flirting on the side. He convinces himself that he does not really have a problem, after all, he is only talking and even if something happens, everybody else is doing it. He will be different, he is nothing like his father. In my experience, that generally does not work out very well. I describe this as an attempt to unconsciously try to fix my parent's behaviour without renouncing the behaviour.

Think that you are too strong to get stuck like those in your past did. So you have an alcoholic parent and you say you can drink and you will be fine; and addiction sneaks up on you because you essentially tried to _**fix**_ your parents' problems without first forgiving them and calling on God's grace. And whatever lessons you do not learn, you pass on to the next generation.

The Power of Negative Baggage or Bondage

It works a lot like this. Basically, you looked at how your father treated your mother and that was your first lesson of how a _**real man**_ treats a woman. If he was disrespectful, or abusive, or left home, then that was your first lesson of what _**real man**_ does. And you looked at how you are your mother treated your father and this was your first lesson of how a woman treats a _**real man**_. Hopefully, if the actions were negative, you have recognized and rejected this image; if not, if you were a boy, you may unconsciously become like your father or find someone who treats you the way your mother treated your father; and if you were a girl, you very likely have lived with a man who treated you the way your father treated your mother.[6]

It can also work the other way around. If you were a girl and you saw your mother abandoned by an unfaithful father, you may have decided that you will not be cheated on, or you will not be hurt and so you are the one causing

---

[6] Note that just because you were raised in an abusive relationship does not mean that you will become abusive yourself. Studying family cycles helps us understand why we see some patterns, but even without ever having done this programme, you may have already decided to be a different person from what you learned from home.

48

the pain in another person's relationship. In other words, a woman can become like her father man like his mother.

The baggage we carry can be both gifts as well as curses. If we are conscious of them, we can enforce the good and work to let go of the bad. The problem is, in my experience, most people do not take the time to recognise what they are bringing into the family with them. This may not seem to be a problem, but I have found that it is often easier to practice the negative that we have seen and heard, then it is to do the positive. So, if you are not conscious of what you are carrying, the chances are, what you do not know is crippling your relationship.

Some of the most obvious examples of baggage is when I see patterns such as addiction, physical and emotional abuse, teenage pregnancy, absent parents (most usually fathers), marital infidelity and divorce and separation. When I deal with people hurting with these issues, the first question I often ask is, "What was your family or origin, or the family of origin of your partner like?" In other words, what baggage are you carrying? Because if you, or your partner, do not let go of the baggage, it does not matter if you change relationship. You will still be carrying the very thing that killed your last encounter and it may do the same in the present. And if you do acknowledge what you are carrying, there is a chance that you can salvage your present relationship.

The Example of Slavery

Even before I start this section, I want to note that it is a simplified example from the Saint Lucian context. It does not take into account all the different racial groups, political factors, but only the predominant group's experience. You may be from a different part of the world with a different history. The history itself is not as important; the critical thing is the learned lesson.

If we do not know how a thing started, or why it exists, we may be doing things that have become acceptable by culture, but that are just as dangerous to us now as when they first began. While I was in seminary, a lecturer once remarked that in the Caribbean, we as Church, have yet to do anything significant to heal the pain of slavery. This is what began my interest in generational baggage.

Why is it becoming more and more difficult to find a man in the Caribbean who thinks it is virtue to be faithful and responsible to only one woman? When I was growing up, I used to hear that black people were hot-blooded and so they could not be faithful spouses nor could they be celibate as they lacked self-control; and ironically, I used to hear this from black people. Interestingly enough, many priests from Africa who come to do ministry in Saint Lucia, wonder why the Church tolerates such behaviour, which means that it is not a natural part of their culture? Even in schools, when I speak about marriage, some teenagers think it must be boring to be living with the same woman for the whole of one's life. And when you do find a young man who is prepared to be faithful, friends make fun of him and think that something is wrong with him. And worst of all, I have had instances where some teenage girls who ridicule boys in class who express interest in remaining faithful to their spouses for life.

So where did it start? Well, here is a little history lesson: during the days of slavery, slaves from the same geographic area and language were separated. Family was discouraged and if a man were to try to settle down, he or his mate could be shipped to another plantation, or the master would come in a rape the woman in front of the man. The reason was very simple: divide and control. If family was tolerated, the slaves could more easily rise in rebellion. Besides, with an ever flowing stream of workers, there was no need to think of sustaining the population.

After the abolition of the Trans-Atlantic slave trade, slave owners and masters began to see the importance of having an available labour supply. The strongest, most handsome men were often taken as studs, to produce children for the plantation. For us looking back, that may seem harsh and depraved, but for these men, it was a privilege. They were treated better than other males who were not as strong and they basically lived a life of pleasure. This meant that the family structure was compromised as the father was not expected to be in the home to instruct and defend. The slaves were therefore less likely to revolt against their condition.

Well, almost two hundred years after emancipation, we kept the tradition of irresponsible fathers. And the effects are the same today. The family is weakened and cycles of poverty and pain continue. Many young persons grow up without knowing their father and are quite resentful of the man who abandoned their family. Today, Father's Day is simply a formality; nobody takes it seriously. By and large, society still upholds the schizophrenic, faulty image of the man: in our commercials and in our movies, the real man is the macho man who thinks about himself and uses others for his own gain; on our talk shows when men are being bashed, the real man is supposed to be responsible and faithful, loving his family. And this affects not only our boys, but also our girls because the men we produce today are the spouses they will have tomorrow. We will keep having broken men until we stop glorifying irresponsibility in private and bashing the irresponsible in public.

If you do not think that fathers are really important in the lives of their children, if you want to know how necessary the father is, just go to any prison or go stand on the block. I worked in a poor community and I also did my thesis on Prison Ministry so I know why there are more males in prison than females. When you interview the young men in prison or those liming on the block, many do not know who their father is; others know his name but have no relationship with him. I have yet to find a single case of a young man being in prison or on the block who had a good relationship with his father. They may be prepared to die for their mothers, but they have a low opinion of their fathers. And some other person, often the gang-leader or drug dealer, took interest in them and made them feel special: the gang leader became the father and they will die for him.

Facing Your Past

What was your family like? What demons did they struggle with? What skeletons did they carry around with them? Many persons do not like to face these issues. In fact, it is possible that not even your spouse knows some of the things you had to go through. Maybe you were too ashamed of your past to share it fully. But you past is killing you right now. Skeletons do not just migrate from our closets; they must be exposed and then buried properly. If you do not face you past consciously, you will be doomed to carry it. And even sadder, you may pass it on to your children.

When it comes to negative baggage, or bondage, the rule is, if you do not face it, it gets worse. So you now stand at the crossroads: you can either take the path to healing, which will be painful now but yield amazing freedom in the future, or you can keep on the path that you are on right now, which will be not as painful now, but only grows more painful later. Choose wisely: your life, your happiness, your family, your children and your future are all in the balance. No stress.

Exercise: Recognising the Bondage

1. Were there things that your parents or other family members did that hurt their relationships or that hurt you directly? Write down who they were and the things that they did (ways of thinking and ways of acting) that hurt your parents' relationship?

   e.g. Temper problems, alcohol or drug addiction, physical abuse…

   _____

   _____

   _____

   _____

2. Write down the negative things that you should not like to do like them in your relationships.

   e.g. I do not want to be unfaithful to my partner, I

do not want to take family for granted…

_____

_____

_____

3. Other people, such as neighbours, friends, or even television personalities, have left us examples by their own lives. What negative experiences or painful life lessons did I have from persons other than my parents?

_____

_____

_____

_____

4. What are the negative things that your parents did that you find yourself or your spouse now doing?

_____

_____

_____

_____

This section may be difficult, but if you can acknowledge the weaknesses that you may be bringing into the relationship, as well as the strengths, then you own them. If you own them, you can control them. If you don't, you may become those weaknesses, or they will follow you. If you will not face the darkness, it does not go away; it only becomes more frightening.

When the exercise is complete, everyone can pray the prayer of renunciation together.

Prayer to Renounce the Burdens Received

Lord Jesus, there are many gifts that I received from my family, but there are also burdens. My parents, or the significant adults in my life, may not have always known how to act. Lord, it is easy for me to ignore the pain and hurt in silence because I do not always trust that others will understand. But I do not want to keep carrying this burden in my life. I do not want to pass this on to my children. I want to be free to live my life as the best father/mother/husband/wife that I can be.

Lord Jesus, help me to love my father and mother. While I should not make excuses for what they did that hurt me, help me to realise that if I do not forgive them, I will become like them. Forgiveness may not be easy, but it is for me. Please take away all my anger and any hatred that may be in my heart. Please remove all fear and anxiety that I may be wrestling with. Lord Jesus, set my heart free to be filled with love and mercy this day. Amen.

Chapter 4:

Breaking the Bondage I: Breaking Free from the Past

If My people, called by My name, humble themselves and pray, repent of their sins and seek My face, then I will hear from heaven. I will forgive their sins and heal their land

(2 Chronicles 7:14).

How do you Move On from the Past

Imagine for a moment, God forbid, that one of your parents was a notorious criminal. And imagine that he or she was killed by police. This would be a truly traumatic event, not just at the moment that your parent died, but everywhere you go afterwards, as soon as people hear your name, especially if you carry that parent's surname, and as soon as they make the connection, they would begin to look at you with suspicion. Even if you were the most law-abiding citizen, you would be carrying the societal bondage of your parent. There would be some opportunities that would automatically be closed to you, even before you ever apply. And imagine how some people, while pretending to give you a fair chance, would just be waiting for you to fall; then they can say that you are just like your father or mother. Well, the reality is, even if this scenario were true, the person you would have to fear the most would be yourself. You need to give yourself permission to rise beyond your past.

This is an extreme instance of the effect of negative baggage; but in all our lives, we can carry the effects of our ancestors' faults. The one thing I do not want you to do as you have been reading this section is thinking that you are stuck where you are. Do not think that your parents' mistakes is going to determine your life; if you want to, you can be free. From this moment onwards, you cannot blame your parents for anything in your life right now. If you blame anyone else other than yourself, you will not be able to move on; that person will always be responsible for the type of person you become. And no matter how painful your past, you are not to think that anyone in your past is responsible for your life.

Now, I am saying this knowing that you may have had extremely painful memories. You may have been the victim of terrible abuse. You may even carry severe physical wounds. These wounds may never go away or they may never heal completely. This may be the hardest thing you have ever had to do in your life, but if you do not choose to move beyond what was done to you, you will not get better.

I think of the example of someone in a traffic accident; she was a very careful and considerate driver but she was hit by a drunk driver. She was pinned in her car and the car caught on fire; she had severe burns all over her body. She was in a coma for a few weeks and had to learn to walk all over again. In such a case, I would understand if she chose not to forgive; I would understand if the pain of learning to walk was too much for her. I would understand if she was confined to a wheelchair for life. I would understand why she chose to stay there and I would feel sorry for her. But I would also know that she did not have to stay there. It would take heroic effort, but she can choose to face the pain and walk again. She can choose to let go of the bitterness and become a joyful person again. And while examples of such persons are rare, they do exist. We call them, Nelson Mandela, Mahatma Ghandi, Mother Theresa, Martin Luther King Jr. We call them Gordon Wilson, whose daughter was killed in an IRA bomb blast on 8th November 1987.[7] He went on to quite openly forgive his attackers and ask that there be no violence in his name. Many people never forgave him for this, but in Ireland today, there is peace, largely because of his efforts.[8] And

---

[7] "Gordon Wilson, 67, Campaigner For Peace in Northern Ireland." Obituaries. The New York Times. June 28, 1995. http://www.nytimes.com/1995/06/28/obituaries/gordon-wilson-67-campaigner-for-peace-in-northern-ireland.html. Web.

I am meant to forgive, even if the person in my past does not repent or is dead. Otherwise, my heart, my emotions, my thoughts, my family, my future will be forever bound to them.[9]

Recognising the Pain of the Past[10]

Exercise I

The most important part of the process of healing and moving on is forgiveness. **Moving on is impossible if there is no forgiveness**. You may want to say this out loud a few times just so that you will hear it. Too many people seem to think that moving on is possible if we just do not talk about the issues; they think that avoiding the

---

[8] "Interviewing Gordon Wilson was nearest I'd ever get to being in presence of a saint." Sunday Life. Belfast Telegraph Digital. October 5, 2008. http://www.belfasttelegraph.co.uk/sunday-life/interviewing-gordon-wilson-was-nearest-id-ever-get-to-being-in-presence-of-a-saint-28491343.html. Web.

[9] Johann Christoph Arnold. Why Forgive. The Plough Publishing Company. 2010. Pg 47. Print.

[10] Another exercise that can be done at this time is a genogram; this however may take a lot of time. Also, the aim of the exercises is not to focus on the brokenness of the past, but to recognize it and move on.

issue is a sign that they have forgiven. If there is anything that you cannot talk about, not even with your spouse, this probably means that this is an area of pain that you need to forgive.

If you are in pain, even if you are the best pretender in the world, there will inevitably be pain in your relationships; the pain must go somewhere. It may manifest in that you find it hard to forgive, or you do not trust easily, or you become easily defensive. You may be afraid of standing up for yourself, or you may have a tendency to hurt others feelings easily. You may be easily depressed, or even (and I found this one very interesting when I noticed it) you can become sick whenever there is conflict in relationships around you. When this happens, you should go through a process of healing or the relationship becomes strained and even damaged.

1. What are some of the things that have been done to me (by parents or other significant persons) that cause me pain whenever I remember, even to this

day? You can use *Appendix I: A Guide for Forgiving Those who Hurt Us* to assist you with this reflection.

_____

_____

_____

2. Are there things that happened to me in the past that I am afraid to remember, that I have not shared with anyone else?

_____

_____

_____

3. How do those things affect my relationships today?

_____

_____

_____

Use the answers from the above exercise to work through the next two part exercises in this simple process. You can also use he answers to the other chapters. *The first step is the letter writing.*

Exercise II: Letter Writing

Write a letter to a parent or someone who hurt me (whether they are alive or dead). If the person is alive, then on the envelopes provided, you may wish to place the address so that the letter can be sent to the person as indicated. If the person is dead, then you can place the name but no address. Use the following as a guideline to your letter.

1. Begin your letter by affirming the other person

   If it is a family member, especially a parent, a sibling, or a former spouse, first tell them that you wish to love them. If you are not yet at this point, then tell them that it is hard because you still feel angry, but be honest while being affirming.

   Let the person know that he or she is God's child. Even if he or she hurt you, God still loves him or

*her and wants to have a relationship with him or
her.*

2. Thank them for the good things they gave you.
   *Thank the person for any good things that he or
   she brought into your life, no matter how small or
   insignificant it may be.*

3. Forgive them for anyway they may have hurt you.
   *Note some things that the person did which caused
   you pain. Write in this way: "When you did...
   (what did the person do), I felt hurt".*

   *Then say how it made you feel about yourself. You
   can use this format: "I felt like... (what did you
   think about yourself)".*

   *Now tell the person that you forgive him or her, if
   you are at that place, and why want to you forgive.
   If you cannot yet forgive, tell them that you are
   trying and praying to get to this place. For me, the
   most important reasons to forgive are that if you
   do not forgive, you cannot heal and move on, and*

if you do not forgive, God will not forgive you (Matthew 6:14-15).

Ask God to bless him or her and grant peace to his or her heart.

4. End you letter by reaffirming that he or she is a child of God and therefore a good person. *He or she may not have acted as God's child, but God wants to forgive him or her and have a relationship with him or her.*

Once everyone has written the letter, move to the third exercise of the process. I recommend that you can have the participants close their eyes and one person guides everyone in the prayer. Have the participants repeat after you. Feel free to add to or remove from the prayers as necessary. You can have some soft music playing in the background, or a worship team doing a song of ministry between each prayer. Note that this prayer is powerful even if parents, grandparents and other significant persons have already died.

If you notice that persons are finding it difficult to go through this prayer journey, then, without disrupting the other participants, they can be lead outside and prayed with and counseled.

Exercise III: Healing and Deliverance Prayer Process

1. *The first step is to be willing to make a full surrender of yourself and your entire life over to the Lord. The Bible tells us that we first have to be fully submitted to the Lord before we can begin to resist the devil to make him flee from us (James 4:7-8). Pray this prayer, or one like it, honestly and deeply; feel free to pray it as often as you need:*

   Lord Jesus, I surrender my heart, my life and my soul completely to you. I ask you to be my Lord. I give you full control. Jesus come into my heart and take control. I belong to you. Amen.

2. *Now, go before the Lord and confess out the sins*

of the parent or parents (the answers to the exercise above).

Lord Jesus, I ask you to forgive my parent/grandparent/ancestor for the ways that they hurt me, especially by the sins of *(honestly confess all the issues of the ancestor [s] who hurt you)*. Lord Jesus, I ask you to forgive. You died on the cross for us; I nail these painful actions to your cross. Jesus have mercy.

I ask forgiveness for anyone who may have been hurt by members of my ancestry, for whatever reason; I also ask your mercy for all those who have hurt members of my family line. Lord Jesus, I symbolically place your holy cross between them as a sign of healing, so that all ill will may be cancelled and only blessing may flow between them. And may your Precious Blood dissolve all hurt and cancel all bad blood. Amen.

3. Now, be willing to fully forgive your parents, or

other persons who hurt you, for whatever they have done to you - no matter how bad or how vicious the abuse has been over the years. Even if you find it hard, remember, you never recover, you never move on unless you first forgive.[11]

In the name of Jesus, I forgive *(name the parent/ancestor whom you wish to forgive)* **for the pain that has been caused to me by their actions. Whether or not they were aware of what they were doing, I will not carry the pain, the guilt and the shame anymore. In the name of Jesus, I renounce all unforgiveness, anger and hatred. I take authority over anger, unforgiveness and hatred and I cast it at the foot of the cross of Jesus.**

4. Sometimes, ancestors may have been involved in things related to the occult or satanism.[12] In this

---

[11] Why Forgive. Pg 31.

[12] As a general rule, whenever I have to write of the evil one, I do not capitalize his name, as a symbol that he is not God, nor is he a rival to God's authority. He may make lots of noise, but he is merely a creature and his power is limited.

case, our struggle is not just with physical habits, but actual demonic strongholds. We now break the connections of curses that demons may have been operating and feeding on over all of those years.

In the name of Jesus, I break all pathways of curses and doorways of bondage between myself and my parents, grandparents and any other ancestors. I place the cross of Jesus between us so that no non-blessing may ever come across from them to me, or from me to them again. Lord Jesus, empower my guardian angel, and the guardian angels of my ancestors, to encourage, strengthen and protect us from all the attacks of the evil one and set us free.

In the name of Jesus, if there are any spirits that were not sent by Jesus, any spirits who act in opposition to His sovereignty, I command you to leave my heart, my soul and my life and never return. All you spirits of *(have persons quietly say whatever bondage they have been wrestling with, those things that are written in the* *exercise above),* **I send you to Jesus for Him to deal with you. I wash myself clean in the Blood of Jesus; I want nothing more to do with you, my life belongs to Jesus. I take authority over you in the name of Jesus, bind you and cast you at the foot of the cross of Jesus for Him to deal with you. In the name of Jesus, leave and do not return. Amen.**

At the end of this prayer process, persons will be asked to place their letters in the special place provided for them. If there will be a Mass or service at the end of the retreat, there can be a time when persons bring the names to the altar and pray for those who hurt them.

Chapter 5:

Breaking the Bondage II: Embracing my Present

No need to remember the past; see, even now I am doing a new thing (Isaiah 43:18,19).

Living Now

The past few exercises have focussed on how the past has largely, for better or worse, influenced the person you are today. Going through these exercises, you may have concluded that your past was so messed up and you may be feeling sorry for yourself. Or you wish that your spouse and children could see how badly you were hurt so that they would excuse you for all the bad decisions you made. Well, good news: self-pity is not an option. No matter how badly you were hurt, the only reason why we made the necessary journey of the past is so that you can see what areas you need to take responsibility for. And that is what we have to do now.

We will explore this question more fully when looking at goals, but, are you happy with the person you have become in life at this point. All of life is a journey, and the decisions that you made are the roads you travelled on. You need to be honest and accept the fact that those decisions have led you to a particular place: now. If you do not like where you are, realise that it is not your parents or your past, nor the abuses that you suffered, no matter how deep. It is you and your choices. If you look carefully, I am sure you can find one person who has gone through the experiences you went through, but who did not end up where you are right now. So now, it is time to change the direction of your life, the direction of your fatherhood and motherhood; the direction of your husband-hood and wife-hood (do not worry if these words do not appear in your dictionary. I may be writing my own dictionary soon).

Essentially, what happens is that we often forget that our life at present is a gift. We live in the past where there was pain, or where we were not loved; and we bring all this pain and unlove into our present family relationships. It is so sad seeing persons who have a spouse or partner who loves them dearly, throw it all away, not only because they have not dealt with their past, but because they have not consciously decided that they will not live the way they used to any more. It is sad seeing someone walk away from his or her children because of the pain of not being able to commit; his or her experiences of parents' commitments were not always favourable and so fear takes over. It is sad, because you do not have to live that way anymore.

Sometimes, persons may want to change, but change is scary. There is often the fear that if I change, I will have to acknowledge that I was wrong; and that will make me look small. Or if I change, persons may use my mistakes against me. If I acknowledge that I was wrong, my children and spouse will not respect me. The truth is, all these excuses are lies. If acknowledging that you were wrong makes you look small in some people's eyes, it is because these people have a low sense of personal value and are trying to prove to others that they are perfect. Besides, the longer you take before acknowledging that you were wrong, the harder it will be when you finally come out and the smaller you will look. Those who would use your mistakes against you are persons who do not want others to see the mistakes that they themselves have done. You are merely the scapegoat. But if you continue to become a better person, after a while, people will see them for what they truly are. And, in my experience, spouses and children actually lose respect for you when you have an attitude that you are always right; besides, if you are always right, it means that everyone else is always wrong if ever they disagree with you. Not really a prerequisite for the father or mother of the year award in my opinion.

Do not be afraid of making mistakes. Do not be afraid of being wrong every now and then. But also, do not be afraid of apologising and moving on. If you cannot see anything wrong in your life, then you should be terrified because that means that there is no room for improvement. And if your family is not the joyful and peaceful place that it ought to be and there is nothing in you that can be improved, it means that your family is stuck in the cycle of pain until you realise that each person is responsible for where the family is right now. If someone placed a hidden camera in your home for a week, would you be proud of what your co-workers would see? If the parish priest or local pastor came to spend a week in your house, would you have to change the way you speak to your family members, hide some magazines, quickly change the television station?

Or then again, if you were told by your doctor that you had only one more month to live, would you begin to treat family differently in any way? What would you want them to say at your eulogy? If I do not change, where will my family be in the next few years? Will we be happy together, or will my children even want to see me? Will I be happily married or will there be a lot of animosity in my relationship? Is being right really worth that much to me?

Exercise I

1. How would I feel if co-workers and fellow church goers found out how I was treating my family members now? Would they approve of the way I speak to them and the things I say?

2. What are the things I know that I need to change in my treatment of family members?

   _____   _____

   _____   _____

   _____   _____

   _____   _____

   _____   _____

3. Are there things that your spouse or children complain about you?

_____   _____

_____   _____

_____   _____

_____   _____

4. What are the reasons that I keep doing those
   negative things?

   _____

   _____

5. If I were honest with myself, are these reasons
   really valid? Is there anyone who has gone through
   the same experiences that I have and who did not
   choose the path that I chose?

6. If _I_ do not change, describe where this will lead
   my family in the next ten years?

   _____

   _____

   _____

Letter Writing Exercises

Exercise II: A letter to self

Before starting this exercise, one person in each group can read the scripture excerpt of Luke 15. Afterwards, the group leader should encourage the members that they are now at a point where, if they want to, they can heal and transform their families through the following exercises. The experience may be difficult, but it can be extremely liberating. The following guidelines can be used in designing the letter to self.

1. Begin your letter by affirming yourself

   You may not think that you deserve it, as you may not think that you are a good person, but remind yourself that you are a child of God. God wants you to come back home; no more excuses. First tell yourself that you wish to love and forgive yourself.

2. Acknowledge some of the good things that you have done for family and loved ones

No matter how small, and no matter how long ago, and no matter how it was received, recognise some of the ways you have shown love to family and loved ones.

3. Forgive yourself for anyway you may have hurt loved ones, both intentionally and unintentionally
Note some of the things you did which caused pain. Sometimes, they were not done with the intention of causing hurt, or sometimes, no one ever found out about these little things that you did, but they still bother you, or they should bother you if you have not acknowledged that you were wrong.
How did doing these things make you feel about yourself? How do you think they made the persons affect feel about you?

4. End your letter with a commitment to become better
Now promise yourself that you will become a better father or mother, spouse or child. Promise

yourself that you will continually ask God for the grace to become better and to never take your family for granted.

Exercise III: A letter to family

For this part of the exercise, the participant will write a letter to each member of his or her family: spouse and children. Depending on how large the family is, this may take at least half an hour or even more, depending on the emotional state of the writer. Even then, it is a very important step; in many cases, this will be the first time the participant will have shared deeply with his or her family in many years.

As far as possible, the letter is not to be used to get back at the other members of the family, or to judge or criticise them; the only person whose sins the participant should focus on is his or her own. If everyone does this, then we will each confess to each other how we have been responsible for the pain in our family and what we can do to make it better, instead of what the other person has done and should do.

To prepare for this session, someone can read Ephesians 5:21-6:4. Persons can then reflect on whether they are treating their family members the way Christ expects them to.

1. Begin the letter by affirming the other person

   Begin by telling the other person that he or she is a good person and a child of God. This may be difficult if you have not paid each other a complement in a long time, but it is so important if you are going to turn your relationship around.

2. Thank the other person for the good things they have done for you.

   Find at least three good things that the other person has done, or that he or she does either for you, for the family, or for others that you are proud of. No matter how small these things are, thank him or her for doing it.

3. Apologise for the way you hurt them.

   Is there anything you did that took family for granted? Or is there anything that caused pain to the other person? Even if you had good intentions, if it caused pain, have the courage to acknowledge it, apologise (which means saying, "I and sorry that I did...") for it and ask the other person to forgive you.

   Now, promise to do your best to become a better father or mother, or husband or wife.

4. Promise to forgive them for anything that may have hurt you

   Promise to forgive him or her for any way that you have been hurt in the past.

   You do not need say how you were hurt, if it is not necessary; choose to put the issue behind you. But if the issue still affects you, you can say what the other person did, how it made you feel. Do not judge the other person as you may not know what was going on in their hearts at the time;

remember, we only intentionally cause pain to others when we are in pain ourselves.

5. Reaffirm that you love him or her and that he or she is a good person
   Remember, you can never say, "I love you," and mean it, too many times. The more you profess your love, the more it grows in your own heart first and the more the other person can believe what you say.

6. End your letter with a promise to pray for him or her
   Promise to place him or her in God's hands and to continually, hopefully daily, ask God to bless and protect him or her.

Exercise IV: A letter to God

1. Thank God for the good things in your life.
   Take the time to list out some of the personal and

family blessings that you should be thankful for. See if you can list at least ten (10) things.

2. Apologise for the way you hurt God by taking His graces for granted.

   *Note some of the things you did that took God and family for granted (**see the examination of conscience in Appendix II** for assistance).*

3. Ask for the grace to be the best that you can be

   If there is any virtue that you need more of, such as patience, humility, or service, ask God to show you how to build these graces in your daily and family life. And ask God to help you to be a better man/woman in the future, especially for your family.

If possible, after the session, the Sacrament of Reconciliation can be made present. After all those who desire have gone to confession, persons may wish to present the letter to their family members. It may be useful to have a counsellor present to assist each couple who wants it as the thoughts expressed on the letter may have been a long time coming and persons may be afraid of sharing, or of how the other person may respond.

Chapter 6:
Moving On

Summary of this workshop: What Baggage are you Carrying

If you made it to the end of this section, the good news is that this was the most difficult section of the programme, but it is so crucial that it had to be done first. Hopefully, you will begin to see a tremendous improvement in your family relationships, as you understand more clearly why you do some of the things you think normal. And hopefully, you will be empowered to break from some of the old behaviours that cause pain to yourself and your relationships.

Recall that baggage, as I define it, is the collection of meanings, attitudes, virtues and vices that you picked up when you were younger, especially from your family of origin, the family that you were born into, that you now carry with you in life. This baggage affects how you relate to relationships at work, on the street, and especially if you are in a romantic relationship, with your partner. Baggage of itself is a neutral concept: it can be both negative and positive.

All baggage, whether negative or positive, often work unconsciously. That means that we often do not stop to think about why we act in this specific way or whether it is right or wrong. The problem with baggage is that because it is unconscious, we do not always see its full effect on our lives. If it is positive, we cannot explain to our peers and children why these attitudes and behaviours are right. If it is negative, we may think that it is natural and pass on cycles of pain to those whom we are close to.

Remember also, while we receive lessons from our past, we are not bound by our past. We can choose to let go and move on at any time, provided that we are conscious of what we are holding on to. This process may be very painful, but the pain of the guilt and shame caused by ignoring cycles of hurt and not choosing to forgive, can sometimes be far greater.

Exercises and further reading

Because of the nature of this book, I recommend that after each section, the family take some time to make the material a part of its life. That means, do not move on to Section II right away. Give yourself a few weeks to a month to live out each part and see how your family changes when the way you think changes. I recommend that as you prepare for the next section, you can do the following things.

Firstly, if there were any members of your family who were not present at the seminar, meet with them and present at the seminar and present their letters to them. You can do this exercise in the presence of the other members of the family, as a sign that you wish to move on and be the best parent/spouse/sibling/child that you can be for the family.

Secondly, be more conscious of the way you treat the members of your family. See if there is any relation between how you treat them and how you saw your parents, or significant adults, treat their families. See also how much you can change negative behaviours and habits. Continuously review the exercises, especially with family members, so that you can chart your progress together. This is one of the easiest ways of being accountable to each other and accountability is a powerful tool for growing in maturity.

A third recommendation is, if you are Catholic, do the prayer journey of *The Family Set Free*. This is a twelve (12) day prayer process meant to help the family through deliverance and healing.

And remember, your past may hurt you, but it does not need to control you.

Appendix I:

Guide for Forgiving Those who Hurt Us[13]

All of us have experienced pain; you may be thinking that in your case, this is the understatement of the year, but we will get to that later! We have all had people that we loved or trusted, but who failed us. Sometimes, we were able to move past their hurt. Sometimes, we get stuck in anger and bitterness. Sometimes, the consequences are so small that the action is hardly noticeable. And sometimes, we have to carry emotional, and even physical scars for the rest of our lives. Sometimes, the pain comes easily to mind; and

---

[13] Adapted from *The Family Set Free: A Journey of Deliverance and Healing*. By Fr. Cleophus Joseph. CreateSpace Independent Publishing Platform. 2016. Pgs 124-132. Print.

sometimes, we have buried it so deeply into our past that it is hard to bring to consciousness.

I know only two realities about pain. Firstly, pain does not need to destroy your life. If you face it, especially with the help of supportive and loving friends and family members, the thing that may have been meant for your destruction can become a means of healing for others. And secondly, the pain that you will not face will only become a cancer eating away at your soul.

For some who may have gone through very difficult traumatic situations, if you cannot go through this alone, then I recommend that you review this process with someone supporting you. But there is no lasting freedom, no lasting happiness, until we choose to forgive and heal... without forgiveness, our hearts and souls wither.[14]

Prayer to Forgive those who Hurt Me

Lord Jesus, I forgive ____ and I ask that you not hold this

---

[14] Johann Christoph Arnold. Seventy Times Seven: The Power of Forgiveness. Plough Publishing House, 1997. 30, xv.

sin against him/her.

O Blood and water which gushed from the Heart of Jesus as a fountain of mercy for us, I trust in You (3x).

Journey of Discovering Those who Hurt Me

<u>From the moment of conception</u>

Although you do not remember this time, but you may have been told stories by your parents or guardians. As you consider the following, forgive all those who may have been involved: parents, grandparents, doctors, teachers, and especially yourself.

- <u>Did your parents' families approve of their relationship</u>? Forgive your parents' families for not accepting them and you.
- <u>Did anyone suggest to your parents that they have an abortion</u>? Forgive that person, whoever they were, for not valuing your life.

- Did your mother think about or try to have an abortion? Forgive your mother; God values you enough to have kept you alive.

- Did the relationship between your father and mother change for the worse when you were conceived? Did they argue a lot? Forgive your parents for not working things out better. And forgive yourself; realise that it was not your fault.

- Did your father abandon the family because you were conceived? Forgive your father and realise that though father and mother leave you, God would never forsake you (Psalm 27:10).

- Were your parents involved in drugs or alcohol while you were in the womb? Sometimes, this may have an effect on you later on. Forgive them so that you may not be bound by drug addiction.

At birth and as a toddler (0-3 years)

- Did one parent feel supported by family and his/her partner? Forgive the unsupportive parent and the rest of the family for not valuing the other person and you?

- Did family and friends make you feel unwelcome? Did family and friends promise to help support the family and then turned back on their word? Forgive them for not receiving you as a gift.

- Did you have other siblings who thought that you were stealing their attention? Forgive your sibling for thinking you had stolen their place. Forgive yourself if you tried to take their place, and if you didn't forgive yourself if you think that they may have been better off without you.

- Were doctors and/or nurses helpful and kind? Forgive them for not doing their duty with the courtesy that was due.

- Did your parents have the resources (both financial and emotional) to give you a normal childhood? Forgive them and realise that they could not give you what they did not have.

- Did people take advantage of your parents, making them do shameful things (such as carry drugs, or exchange sexual favours) in exchange for assistance? Forgive them for using their power over others to cause pain to your family and you.

- Were you ever sick and had to stay in hospital? And did you think that your parents abandoned at that moment? Forgive your parents. Realise how hard that decision must have been on them. And forgive yourself for thinking that they had abandoned you.

- Were your parents responsible persons or did they leave you for extended periods in order to go have fun? Forgive your parents for not growing up.

At the beginning of school (4-5 years)

- On the first day of school, did you feel abandoned by your parents when they left you? Forgive your parents because that moment must have been on them too. And forgive yourself for thinking that they had abandoned you.

- Did you make friends easily? Were the other children mean and insulting? Did you ever get bullied at school or at home? <u>Did friends ever play trick on you that ended up costing you</u>? Forgive your schoolmates. Sometimes, children can say and do the most painful things without even realising and meaning it.

- <u>Were you ever the bully at home or at school? Did you ever play tricks on a friend that ended up costing them</u>? Forgive yourself, because sometimes you did really stupid things without understanding the consequences.

- <u>Did the teacher say things that made you feel bad about yourself</u>? Forgive the teacher (s). Sometimes, adults have personal issues and take them out on children.

- <u>Did you anyone ever tell you, or make you feel like you were not good enough, or that you were stupid or ugly</u>? Forgive them. Your real dignity is found not in their words and actions but in God's words. And forgive yourself for believing them.

<u>From school to early teenage years (6-12 years)</u>

- <u>Were you ever robbed</u>? Forgive the thief; their actions may have made you feel weak and foolish but realise that you are not a foolish person just because someone took advantage of you. They were wrong.

- <u>Did you ever steal from anyone</u>? That was your past. Forgive yourself and choose to be something different in the future.

- <u>Were you abused physically (beaten badly), or verbally (insulted and put down)</u>? No matter how "bad" you were, you did not deserve that. Forgive the abuser and reclaim your dignity as a beautiful, intelligent child of God.

- <u>Was one of your parents/guardians physically abusive to another</u>? This is not the way adults ought to treat each other. Forgive the abusing parent so that you may not follow the cycle of abuse in your own life.

- <u>Was one of your parents/guardians involved in alcohol or drugs</u>? Forgive your parent or guardian for not being able to properly deal with their issues and realise that there is always another way for your life.

- Were you abused sexually, by a parent, guardian, sibling, friend, teacher, neighbour or stranger, religious leader? Forgive this person; realise that you may still need to seek justice so that other children may be protected, or so that part of your life can be restored to normalcy, but forgive and let go of all anger and hatred towards them. And forgive yourself; realise that as a child, you were not responsible for the abuse you suffered.

- Sometimes, abuse may be unintentional; did a friend ever try something they had seen on you? Forgive the person; realise that they did not intend to harm you.

- Did you in any way abuse a sibling, friend, neighbour? Did you ever try anything that you had seen on someone else? Forgive yourself for the foolish things you did in the past. If it is possible, make restitution by at least offering an apology.

- Were you exposed to pornography, on television, on magazines, on the internet, in books? Forgive the persons who exposed you to these images, whether in ignorance or because they were irresponsible themselves. And forgive the actors and models for offering their bodies as a lie when no real relationship would ever result.[15]

- Were you able to understand the work at school? Forgive teachers, parents and schoolmates if they made you feel foolish and forgive yourself if you chose to stop trying.

From Teenage to early Adult Years (13-18)

- Were you ever raped by a boyfriend/girlfriend, sibling, friend, parent, teacher, neighbour, stranger? Did anyone ever force you, whether physically or with threats, to have sex with them?[16]

---

[15] In my experience, I realize that people become addicted to pornography because they are hungry for relationship. But in reality, the person on the screen does not know you, does not love you and does not seek to give themselves to you in a committed relationship.

[16] The second part of the question is added because I have found that many persons actually cannot recognize that they have been raped. Sometimes, the attacker did not use physical violence, or it may have

Forgive the other person for taking something so valuable from you; forgive them for the causing the immense shame that you had to experience later on in life. And forgive yourself if you felt that you were in some way responsible or that you were not strong enough. It does not matter who you were and what you did, you did not deserve to be violated.

- <u>Did you ever force anyone, whether physically or with threats, to have sex with you</u>? Forgive yourself for your stupid decisions. Do your best to let the other person know that you are sorry, because what you took away can never be replaced. And let them know that they have infinite value before God.

- <u>Did your parents argue a lot</u>? <u>Did you sometimes feel that you were responsible for their arguments, that they would be happier if you had never been born</u>? Forgive your parents for not having the courage to deal with their real issues. Realise that

---

been a boyfriend who simply threatened to shame the victim.

there is another way in your own life and relationships.

- <u>Did you feel like you did not belong?</u> <u>Did you ever think about or try to commit suicide?</u> Forgive anyone who may have made you feel bad about yourself. And forgive yourself for not seeing your real value and for trying to take the place of God, the power to give and take not only life but value, in your life.

- <u>Did you have an abortion?</u> Forgive yourself for the decision, whatever the reason. Name the child, place the child in God's hands and ask the child to forgive you and pray for you. Also, forgive the doctors, nurses and all others who had a part to play.

- <u>Did you encourage another person to have an abortion?</u> Forgive yourself for your role in the killing of an innocent child. Recognise the guilt and shame that the mother may be going through: help her to forgive herself, to name her child and place the child in God's hands.

- <u>Did anyone introduce you to alcohol or drugs</u>? Forgive the person (s) and forgive yourself for your stupid decisions.

- <u>Did you and your parents ever get into an argument in front of you</u>? Forgive your parents for not being responsible in their communication to one another and for giving you a bad example.

- <u>Did your parents make you feel like they had no time to listen to you, that your opinions didn't mattered or that they did not know and care about you</u>? Forgive your parents for not making the time to show love and affection. Realise that they may have loved you, but just did not make the time to show it. You can be different in your family.

- <u>Did a boyfriend or girlfriend break your heart</u>? <u>Did they leave you or were they unfaithful</u>? Forgive them for not valuing you for who you are.

- <u>Did you break someone's heart</u>? <u>Were you unfaithful</u>? Forgive yourself for your actions. If possible, ask them to forgive you and remind them that their real value is in God's love for them.

From early adult years to now (19 - now)

- Did you have to face rejection when looking for a job or trying to pursue higher studies? Realise that rejection is a normal part of life. It does cause pain though and for that, you need to forgive those who turned you down, even if they were justified in their decision. And forgive yourself if you chose to give up and stop trying.

- Did you have a spouse or partner who was unfaithful? As you get older, the cost of infidelity is greater, especially if you are in a committed relationship. Forgive the spouse or partner as well as the one with whom they cheated.

- Were you unfaithful to your spouse or partner? Forgive yourself for the pain caused to your spouse and family, and the family of the person you cheated with, if they found out. If they did not find out, forgive yourself and the other person and decide that your family and reputation are worth more to you than these moments of pleasure.

- <u>Did you ever have a divorce or were you separated</u>? Forgive yourself and your spouse for your roles in the event. Especially if there are children involved, decide that even if you and your spouse are no longer together, you cannot hate each other.

- <u>Did you ever wish you could have gotten a divorce because you and your spouse no longer love each other</u>? Forgive yourself and your spouse for not fighting for your relationship (one person may sometimes have greater responsibility in the matter than the other, but both persons must be forgiven).

- <u>Do you make time for your spouse and children and make them feel that they are important to you or are you always too busy</u>? If you are always busy, forgive yourself for not realising that the only place where you are indispensable is your family and make the commitment to change, even if it will be hard.

- <u>Did you lose your job</u>? Forgive your employer, and anyone else involved in your firing. Forgive yourself if you were not a good worker.

- <u>Did you ever experience a reckless or selfish driver</u>? Forgive that driver and recognise that persons sometimes act the way they have been treated by others. You do not have to be the same way; you can choose not to be part of the "rat race".

- <u>Are you a reckless and selfish driver</u>? Forgive yourself and realise that unless you make a difference, things will always be the same.

- <u>Do your workmates gossip about you</u>? Forgive them. People only talk about persons who are important enough to be talked about, so you are worth something.

- <u>Do you gossip about your workmates</u>? Forgive yourself and those whom you gossip with. Realise that you don't need to become like anyone else. You can choose your own path.

109

- <u>Has your house or business place ever been broken into</u>? When your sanctuary is violated, you feel vulnerable, afraid and angry. Forgive the person who did this. Realise that they can only take your inner peace if you allow them to.

- <u>Did anyone ever scam you or take advantage of your good heart</u>? Forgive them and learn from the incident. Forgive yourself, because sometimes, people are able to manipulate us because of our own inner demons (such as the need to be loved by everyone, or having bad boundaries, or the desire to get rich quickly).

- <u>Have you ever scammed anyone or taken advantage of their need</u>? Forgive yourself for your actions. Realise that your actions and choices say what kind of person you are. Decide that you want to be different.

Appendix II:
A Forgiveness Ritual

Rituals provide us a process in which to do something. This in turn makes it easier to think through or understand something. Forgiveness is difficult; one of the ways of making it easier is to have a ritual of forgiveness, a process we go through whenever we are hurt. Here is a simple process that can be used:

1. **Acknowledge the hurt:**

   Pretending that I am okay will not make the pain go away; trying to make excuses for the one who hurt me will not make me heal either. Ask questions like the following:
   - What happened?
   - How did it make me feel about myself?
   - Why do I think the person did this (and do not immediately assume that he or she is

evil. Try to honestly see things from his or her perspective)?

2. Refuse to allow anger and hatred to cloud your heart

When someone hurts us the desire for justice or revenge will always come; but we cannot allow these feelings to remain. If they do, they poison the relationship and begin to affect all the other persons around us. If you do not believe me, try to recall someone who hurt you and try smiling at the same time. You will realise that as long as you think about the pain that he or she caused, this is impossible (unless you are smiling at the thought of the getting back at the person). It is impossible to be truly happy with a heart full of anger, hatred and unforgiveness. Try this process:

-   Think of the person who hurt you.

- Realise that no matter what he or she did and what he or she intended, you are still here.
- Now think the words, "I am a good, beautiful person" a few times.
- Now smile; this works because you are working on your image of yourself. Whenever you are hurt by others, your image of yourself suffers; the more important they are to you, the more you self-image is affected. Acknowledging that you are good and beautiful, while thinking about the other person, takes your mind off the pain that they may have caused, and focuses on the good that you can do. Remember, your actions and thoughts will almost always be consistent with your image of yourself.

3. Reject guilt and shame as well as judging and blaming

Guilt and shame can sometimes keep us stuck in bad relationships; we often feel ashamed because we sometimes think that if we were better, the other person would not hurt us. This is not just for abusive relationships, but every time we get hurt, the first instinct is often to think unconsciously "Something must be wrong with me". If we grew up hearing that we were not good enough, then this will not be so unconscious. Realise that just because someone else did something to you does not make you a bad person. It may help to just say repeatedly, "I am a good person."

Also be aware of the tendency to judge and blame the other. Sometimes, people do deserve blame; we need to say "You did this and you need to take responsibility for your words and actions." That is not the same as, "You are a bad person and you did it because you do not like me." Truth is, I have no idea why you did it; all I know is that it is wrong and it hurt me.

And if you do not accept responsibility and make the decision to change, I will not allow you to stay in my life. You are still a good person, but you need to deal with your issues.

4. Know the difference between a painful situation and an unhealthy relationship

All human relationships experience conflict; we can sometimes feel guilty that there was a disagreement, but if you find yourself always agreeing with someone, that probably means that the other person is a figment of your imagination. Healthy conflict is normal; in healthy conflict, we are not trying to see who is right and who is wrong, but how can we become better in this relationship. This is important, because if your communication, especially in times of conflict, is not healthy, neither is your relationship. If you want to know if the conflict in your relationships are healthy, ask the following questions:

- When there is a disagreement, are we prepared to listen to each other's point of view, or do we both shout at the same time?

- Which is more important, that each person in the relationship is happy or who is right and who is wrong?

- How often do we argue? What do we argue about and how heated do our arguments become (if you find that you are having repeated and heated arguments, especially about the same subjects, it may mean that you need help in your relationship as you are not communicating well)?

- Do we use insults and profanity at each other or do we maintain respect for each other even when we are angry?

5. Bless the other person

Jesus reminds us to pray for those who persecute us (Matthew 5:43-58) and Paul adds that we ought to bless them (Romans 12:14,

17). Forgiveness is difficult, but it helps me when I honestly ask God to bless the one who hurt me. I believe that everyone who hurts me is first in pain themselves. If I increase their pain, the only thing they will be able to do is keep hurting themselves, me and others. So, even if it is hard and I just wish that the other be in pain, sometimes I bless not because I want to, but so that he or she may stop hurting me.

I also believe that whatever I wish for someone else, I end up receiving for myself also. So I refuse to allow someone else to destroy my inner peace and joy, or to make me someone who is bitter and vengeful, or to steal my blessings. For me, forgiveness is not only a Christian act, it is also a selfish act. I want to be blessed and healed, so I will forgive and bless you from my heart. And it makes me feel free when I do this; I truly feel like a better person. So try this little formula or one like it:

- "Lord, I bless (name the person) from my heart and I ask that you bless him/her. I want to become a better person, free of the diseases of hatred and bitterness, so I release all claims of vengeance for what was done to me. Lord have mercy on (name the person) and on me. Amen."

People often think that unforgiveness and hardness of heart make them powerful, but it is quite the opposite. These things strangle our capacity to love and receive love as well as to be happy. It is impossible to be happy with unforgiveness in your heart. You can try all you want, but inevitably one of the two will have to go: your bitterness or your happiness. Some people never realise this.

Appendix III: Examination of Conscience for Families[17]

This examination is based on the Ten Commandments. For the journey, you can write down what your sins are to make it easier to remember. If you are using this examination at other times, you can simply add a short pray, such as, "Jesus, I'm sorry, please forgive me," after each sin that you are guilty of.

I am the Lord Your God... You shall have no other god before me.

- Have I or any member of my family ever been involved with occult and non-Christian religions?

---

[17] Adapted from *The Family Set Free: A Journey of Deliverance and Healing*. Pgs. 121-123.

- To my knowledge, were any members of my family, especially in past generations involved with the occult or non-Christian religions?
- Have I planned my life based on horoscopes, Ouija boards, tarot card readings?
- Have I used charms to try to gain protection or success (e.g. putting things in clothing or the foundation of the house to keep away evil spirits)?
- Have I made any blood pacts or spiritual ties with anyone, especially in gangs?
- Were any members of my family involved in secret societies that may have used blood pacts and spiritual ties?
- Are there things or people that I put before God, such as politics, sports, friends? In other words, if I had a choice between doing something for God (such as praying or attending church service or Mass) and this activity, which would I choose? Would it be a struggle for me to choose God?

You shall not take the Name of the Lord in Vain.

- Have I ever used God's name in a way that was not meant to honour Him (e.g. do I call God's name when I fall, or when things go wrong without intending to honour Him)?
- Do I keep the promises that I make to family members?
- Do I tell lies?
- Do I use foul language, especially against my parents, spouse and/or children?

Remember the Sabbath Day and Keep it Holy.

- Do I go to Mass or other Church services with my family? Do I intentionally miss Mass or Church services on Sundays or days of obligation because of laziness, involvement in other activities, lack of commitment?
- Do I pray at home with my family? Do we make sufficient time for prayer?

Honour your father and mother.

- If I am married, or in a relationship, have I disrespected my spouse or partner, especially in the presence of our children?
- Have I disrespected my parents or children and other family members?
- Have I disrespected other persons of authority?
- Do I make sufficient time for my family?
- Have I been abusive, whether physically (battering), emotionally (causing them to be distressed), verbally (using insults and threats) or sexually?
- Do my children and family members know that I care for them?
- Do I treat my employees or others over whom I have authority with respect?

You shall not kill.

- Am I guilty of murder?
- Am I guilty of negligence in the death or another?

- Do I drive responsibly on the road, especially with family members around?
- Am I guilty of speaking and acting in anger?
- Have I used contraceptives or have had abortions?
- Do I gossip and slander others, especially members of my family?
- Do I judge and condemn others?
- Am I guilty of unforgiveness?
- Do I hate anyone?
- Have I been prejudiced, refusing to show kindness to anyone because of the way they looked, their religion, their gender, or based entirely on what someone else said about them?

You shall not Commit Adultery.

- Am I married and have had an extramarital affair?
- Am I sexually active even if I am not married, and guilty of fornication?
- Do I engage in pornography, reading and looking at indecent material in books, magazines, on television, on computer?

- Do I engage in masturbation?

- Do I tolerate lustful thoughts and desires?

- Do I fail to dress decently and so may lead others into temptation?

- Do I engage in indecent conversations?

- If I am a parent, do I encourage my children to be chaste, not only by my words, but especially by my actions?

- Do I engage in homosexual thoughts and activities?

You shall not steal.

- Have I been guilty of stealing, taking what was not mine without permission?

- Am I guilty of not paying a fair wage to those who serve me?

- Am I guilty of not working properly for my just wages?

- Do I encourage others, especially family members, to be dishonest?

- Do I spend my money in an irresponsible way, and so endanger the future of my family (e.g. Do I gamble away lots of money, or do I spend so much on unimportant things that food, education and shelter may be compromised)?

You shall not covet your neighbour's wife and goods.

- Have I been envious of others because of what they have?
- Have I tried to break up others relationships because of jealousy, wanting to have the spouse or partner of another?
- Have I not been content with what I have; and if I desire more, do I try to gain it by dishonest means?

Bibliography

Arnold, Johann Christoph. <u>Seventy Times Seven: The Power of Forgiveness</u>. Plough Publishing House, 1997. Print.

Arnold, Johann Christoph. <u>Why Forgive</u>. The Plough Publishing Company. 2010. Print.

"Gordon Wilson, 67, Campaigner For Peace in Northern Ireland." <u>Obituaries</u>. The New York Times. June 28, 1995. <u>http://www.nytimes.com/ 1995/06/28/obituaries/gordon-wilson-67- campaigner-for-peace-in-northern-ireland.html</u>. Web.

"Interviewing Gordon Wilson was nearest I'd ever get to being in presence of a saint." Sunday Life. Belfast Telegraph Digital. October 5, 2008. <u>http://www.belfasttelegraph.co.uk/sunday- life/interviewing-gordon-wilson-was-nearest-id- ever-get-to-being-in-presence-of-a-saint- 28491343.html</u>. Web.

Jarema, Fr. William. Clergy Pastoral Institute. Archdiocesan Clergy Retreat. Cardinal Kelvin Felix Archdiocesan Pastoral Centre. September 2012. Talk.

Joseph, Fr. Cleophus. *The Family Set Free: A Journey of Deliverance and Healing*. CreateSpace Independent Publishing Platform. 2016. Print.

Kelly, Matthew. *The Four Signs of A Dynamic Catholic: How Engaging 1% of Catholics Could Change the World.* Beacon Publishing. 2013. Kindle Edition.

McAll, Kenneth. *Healing the Family Tree*. SPCK. Kindle Edition.

SSemakula, Fr. Yozefu. The Healing of Families. healingoffamilies.com. 2012. Print.

52525354R00079

Made in the USA
Columbia, SC
10 March 2019